LET'S LOOK ON THE FARM

HOW TO USE THIS BOOK

Farms change throughout the year. This book is about the animals and plants you are most likely to find on a farm during the spring, summer and autumn months. Use this guide to...

...read about different farm animals and crops and discover what is so amazing about them.

...take outside with you to see what you can find and identify, then tick off the things you see.

...have fun playing with the stickers on the fold-out farm play scene at the back.

Down on the farm

Some farms keep animals such as cows, sheep or even fish. Others grow food such as fruit or vegetables. Here are some of the crops and animals you may see.

Cows and sheep
Look out for them grazing in fields. How many different types can you spot?

Horses
Horses used to pull heavy machinery. Now they are kept mostly for riding.

Pigs and goats
Colourful stamps and ear tags mean farmers can tell their animals apart.

Fruit and vegetables
How much food do you eat? Most of it is grown on farms and transported to shops.

Cereal crops
Can your parents tell the difference between wheat, barley and oats?

Farm birds
Hens, geese, turkeys and ducks are farm birds. They are also called poultry.

Amazing farm facts

Which orange vegetable used to be
purple? What is a hinny? Find
out the answers below.

Cows, sheep and goats need to
have a baby in order to produce milk.

Apples float in water. Pears do not.

Scarecrows are sometimes used to frighten
hungry birds away from tasty crops.

A female horse crossed with a male
donkey is called a mule.

A female donkey crossed with a male
horse is called a hinny.

Cows have four stomachs.

Hens often cluck as they lay their eggs.

The weakest baby animal in a litter
is called the runt.

Carrots were often purple, not orange.

Barn owls make a screeching sound.
They do not hoot.

pig ○

Farm spotters, turn the page!

Easy to spot

You will probably need to visit different types
of farm to find all these plants and animals.

○ pig

○ chick

○ hen

○ cow

farm cats ○

○ rapeseed

barley ○

○ duck

○ wheat

○ sheep

bee ○

○apples

sheepdog ○

lamb

calf ○

oats ○

goat ○

○ cockerel

horse ○

hay bale ○

○ goose

Tick them off as you find them.

Harder to spot

○ lettuce

○ butterfly

strawberries ○

beans ○

○ gosling

○ piglet

pears ○

turkey ○

○ grapes

○ bull

○ donkey

○ kid

plums ○

barn owl ○

○ eggs

guineafowl ○

ram ○

dove ○

cherries ○

maize ○

duckling ○

○ hops

Farmyard families

In the spring, many farmers are busy helping their animals produce their young. Do you know the names for all these farm animals and their babies?

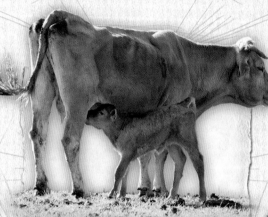

Hens and chicks
A broody hen sits on its eggs for 21 days before the chicks hatch out.

Nannies and kids
Kids can be born all year round. The mother, or nanny, often has two or three at a time.

Cows and calves
Most calves are born in the spring. It is very unusual for a cow to have more than one calf.

Mares and foals
A foal is able to stand up and run around within hours of being born.

Sows and piglets
The mother pig, or sow, can have as many as 14 piglets in one litter.

Ewes and lambs
Ewes usually have between one and three lambs in the springtime.